MW01285149

UNIVERSAL REFERENCE GUIDE

SPACE

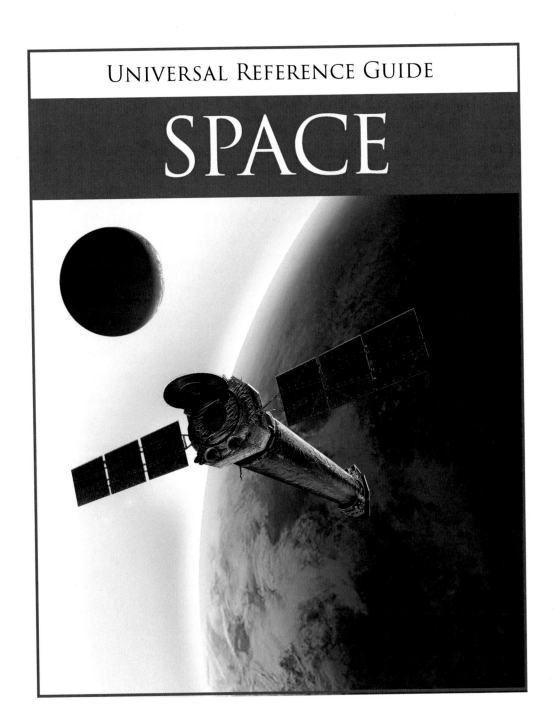

PORTRAIT
LIBRARY

UNIVERSAL REFERENCE GUIDE: **SPACE**

Reference Source:

Britannica

Study.com

Image courtesy:

Inspirock

Alamy

Stock Photos

iStock

Getty Images

Compiled and edited by: NextStage

Published by: Portrait Library

Copyright © Portrait Library

An imprint of NextStage Events and Communication

All rights are reserved and unauthorized production in any manner is prohibited.

Edition: 2024

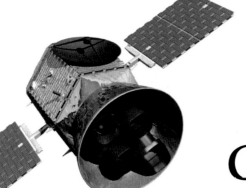

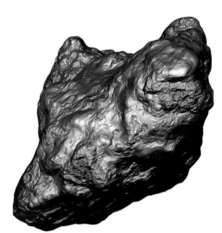

Contents

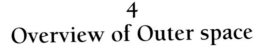

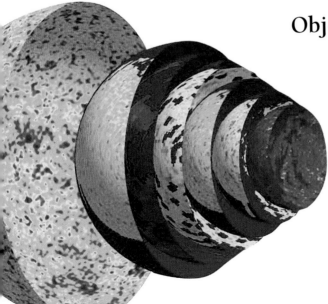

Overview of Outer space

Outer space or space is made up of the relatively empty regions of the universe found outside the atmospheres of celestial bodies. Outer space is the term used to distinguish itself from airspace and terrestrial locations. There is no clear boundary used to differentiate Earth's atmosphere and space. This is because the density of the atmosphere slowly starts to decrease as the altitude increases.

Outer space

Hungarian-American physicist, aerospace engineer and mathematician, Theodore von Karman

For a better understanding, the Federation Aeronautique Internationale has set up what is called the Karman line at a height of 100 kilometers to establish a boundary between aeronautics and astronautics. This line was chosen because Theodore von Karman calculated that a vehicle moving above that altitude would have to move faster than orbital velocity in order to derive enough aerodynamic lift from the atmosphere to support itself.

The United States designates people who travel above a height of 80 kilometers as astronauts. During the re-entry process, approximately 120 kilometers marks the boundary where the atmospheric drag becomes noticeable, based on the ballistic coefficient of the vehicle.

Despite what many believe, outer space is not actually completely empty, i.e., it is not in a perfect vacuum. Instead, outer space contains low density of particles, particularly hydrogen plasma, as well as electromagnetic radiation. According to some theories, outer space also contains dark matter and dark energy.

Outer space provides a challenging environment for human exploration thanks to the hazards of vacuum and radiation. Microgravity also has a negative effect of human physiology. Along with the economic and environmental effects on humans, the economic costs of putting objects into space is very high.

Paradise lost.
A
POEM
Written in
TEN BOOKS
By JOHN MILTON.

Licensed and Entred according to Order.

LONDON

Printed, and are to be sold by *Peter Parker* under *Creed* Church neer *Aldgate*; And by *Robert Boulter* at the *Turks Head* in *Bishopsgate-street*; And *Matthias Walker*, under St. *Dunstons* Church in *Fleet-street*, 1667.

Cover of Paradise Lost, by John Milton in 1667

HOW THE NAME CAME

The term outer space was first recorded by English author H.G. Wells in his novel 'First Men in the Moon' in 1901. The term space dates back much further, used first to mean the region beyond Earth's sky in John Milton's Paradise Lost in 1667.

ENVIRONMENT IN OUTER SPACE

Outer space is the closest natural approximation to a perfect vacuum, i.e., it effectively has no friction, allowing stars, moons and planets to move freely along ideal gravitational trajectories. However, there is no vacuum truly perfect, not even in intergalactic space where there are still a few hydrogen atoms per cubic centimeter. The deep vacuum of space could make it an interesting environment for certain industrial processes but at present, it is much less costly to create a perfect vacuum on Earth than to leave Earth's gravity well.

Stars, planets, asteroids and moons keep their atmospheres by gravitational attraction and as such, atmospheres have no clearly set boundary: the density of atmospheric gas slowly starts to decrease with distance from the object. The Earth's atmospheric pressure drops to about 1 Pa at 100 kilometers of altitude at the Karman line. Beyond this line, isotropic gas pressure rapidly becomes less important in comparison to the radiation pressure coming from the sun and the dynamic pressure produced by solar winds. The thermosphere in this range has large gradients of pressure, temperature and composition and can vary based on space weather. Astrophysicists prefer to use number density in order to describe these environments in units of particles per cubic centimeter.

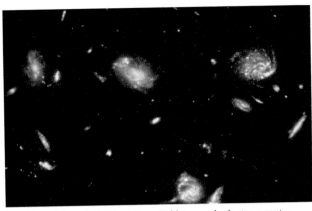

Part of the Hubble Ultra-Deep Field image, displaying a section of space in a deep vacuum

The observable universe is filled with large numbers of photons, the so-called cosmic background radiation and quite likely, a correspondingly large number of neutrinos. The current temperature of this radiation is 3 Kelvins or -270.15° C.

Cold or oxygen-rich atmospheres are able to sustain life at pressures much lower than atmospheric, as long as the density of oxygen is similar to that of the standard sea-level atmosphere. The colder air temperature that is seen at altitudes of 3 kilometers generally compensate for the lower pressure there. Above this altitude, oxygen enrichment is required to prevent altitude sickness and spacesuits are used to prevent ebullism from occurring at 19 kilometers.

Cosmic microwave background or CMB

An astronaut floating in space

Formation and the Big Bang

The Big Bang is the cosmological model of the universe, whose primary assertion is that the current universe expanded to this state from a primordial condition of enormous density and temperature. In a much narrower way, the term is used to describe the fundamental 'fireball' that erupted at or close to an initial time-point in the history of observed spacetime.

One of the many possible interpretations of the Big Bang Event

Theoretical support for the Big Bang comes from mathematical models known as Friedmann models. According to these models, the Big Bang theory is consistent with the theory of general relativity and with the cosmological principle. The latter states that the properties of the universe should be independent when it comes to both orientation and position.

Observational evidence for the Big Bang includes analyses of the spectra of light from galaxies, which reveal a shift towards longer wavelengths proportional to each galaxy's distance in a relationship descried by Hubble's Law. This, combined with the evidence that observers found anywhere in the universe make similar observations, suggesting that space itself is expanding.

Following the initial expansion, the universe then cooled down enough to allow for the formation of subatomic particles, and later atoms. Giant clouds of these primordial elements such as hydrogen, helium and lithium then later coalesced through gravity, to form early stars and galaxies, the descendants of which are visible today. Aside from these early building materials, astronomers also observe the gravitational effects of an unknown dark matter surrounding galaxies.

A cloud of space gas

Georges Henri Joseph Edouard Lemaitre was a Belgian Catholic priest, mathematician, astronomer and professor of physics.

Georges Lemaitre first noted in 1927 that an expanding universe can be traced back through time to an originating single point, which he referred to as the 'primeval atom'. For many decades, the scientific community was divided between those who supported the Big Bang theory and the rival steady-state model. However, a wide range of empirical evidence has strongly favored the Big Bang, which is now universally accepted by both the scientific and non-scientific community.

American astronomer Edwin Hubble confirmed through analysis of galactic redshifts in 1929 that galaxies are indeed drifting apart, which is important observational evidence for an expanding universe. In 1964, the CMB was discovered which was vitally important evidence in favor of the Big Bang model of the universe, as that theory predicted a uniform background radiation found throughout the Universe.

Edwin Powell Hubble, an American astronomer played a crucial role in establishing the fields of observational cosmology and extragalactic astronomy

Close up of a galaxy among many other galaxies

Impression of a Wilkinson Microwave Anisotropy Probe or WMAP

MISCONCEPTIONS

A common misconception about the Big Bang Model is that it fully explains the origins of the universe. However, the model only describes the emergence of the present universe from an ultra-dense and high-temperature initial state. When the size of the universe at the Big Bang is described, it in fact refers to the size of the observable universe and not the entire universe.

STATE OF THE UNIVERSE

The present day shape of the universe was determined through the measurements of cosmic microwave background using satellites like the Wilkinson Microwave Anisotropy Probe. These observations indicate that the spatial geometry of the observable universe is 'flat.' This means that photons on parallel paths at one point remain parallel as they travel through space to the edge of the observable universe. The concept of a flat Universe, combined with the measured mass density of the Universe and the accelerating expansion of the Universe all indicate that space has a non-zero vacuum energy, popularly known as dark energy.

Estimates put the average energy density of the present day Universe at the equivalent of 5.9 protons per cubic meter, including dark energy, dark matter and baryonic matter. These atoms make up for only 4.6% of the total energy density, or a density of one proton per four cubic meters. The density of the Universe is certainly not uniform and ranges from relatively high density in galaxies to conditions in vast voids that have much lower density. Unlike dark matter and matter, dark energy does not seem to be concentrated in galaxies but does account for a majority of mass-energy in the Universe.

Humans and outer space

DISCOVERY

In the year 350 BC, Aristotle, a Greek philosopher suggested that nature abhors a vacuum, a principle that was later called the horror vacui. Greek philosopher Parmenides further built upon the idea by denying the existence of a void in. Based on the idea that a vacuum could not exist, many in the West believed that space could not be an empty void. As late as the 17th century, French philosopher Rene Descartes argued that the entirety of space must be filled.

Portrait of Galileo Galilei

Drawing of Otto von Guericke beside a vacuum pump

In ancient China, 2nd century astronomer Zhang Heng became convinced that space must be infinite, extending well beyond the mechanism that supported the Sun and the stars. The surviving books of Hsuan Yeh School said that the heavens were boundless, empty and void of substance.

Galileo Galilei, the famous Italian scientist knew that air had mass and so was subject to gravity. In 1640, he demonstrated how an established force could resist the formation of a vacuum. After the invention of the first mercury barometer in Europe, French mathematician Blaise Pascal reasoned that if the mercury column was supported by air, then the column should be shorter at higher altitudes, where the air pressure is lower.

In 1650, German scientist Otto von Guericke built the first vacuum pump, a device that furthered the principle of the horror vacui. Through this invention, he concluded that there must be a vacuum between the Earth and the Moon.

In the 15th century, German theologian Nicolaus Cusanus speculated that the Universe did not have a center and a circumference. He believed that the universe was not infinite but could not be termed as finite, as it lacked any bounds within which it could be contained.

Drawing of a bust of Aristotle

QUICK FACTS

The concept of an aether first began with ancient Greek philosophers, including Aristotle, who saw it as a medium through which the heavenly bodies move.

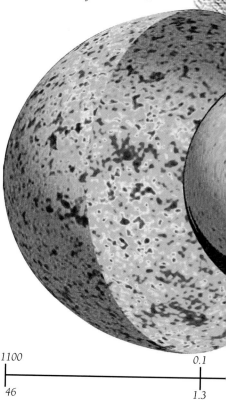

1100   0.1

46   1.3

These ideas led to speculations about the infinite dimension of space by Italian philosopher Giordano Bruno in the 16th century. English philosopher William Gilbert argued that stars are only visible to humans, only because they are surrounded by a thin aether or void.

The idea of a universe filled with a luminiferous aether was supported among some scientists until the early 20th century. In 1887, the Michelson-Morley experiment tried to detect the Earth's motion through this medium. The result indicated that something was wrong with this concept. The idea of luminiferous aether was dropped. It was replaced by Albert Einstein's theory of special relativity, which holds that the speed of light in a vacuum is a fixed constant, independent of the observer's motion or their frame of reference.

The first professional astronomer who supported the idea of an infinite Universe was Englishman Thomas Digges in 1576. However, the scale of the universe remained unknown, until the first successful measurement of the distance to a nearby star in 1838 by German astronomer, Friedrich Bessel.

American astronomer Edwin Hubble determined the distance to the Andromeda Galaxy in 1923. Hubble measured the brightness of Cepheid variables in that galaxy. This technique stabled that the Andromeda galaxy as well as all other galaxies are located well outside the Milk Way.

Portrait of Thomas Digges

The Michelson-Morley experiment, mounted on a stone slab that floats in an annular trough of mercury. Albert A. Michelson and Edward W. Morley performed the experiment between April and July of 1887'

Impression of the Andromeda Galaxy

The modern concept of outer space came from the Big Bang theory, first proposed in 1931 by Belgian physicist Georges Lemaitre.

The earliest known estimate of the temperature of outer space was by Swiss physicist Charles E. Guillaume in 1895. By examining the radiation of the background stars, he concluded that space is heated to a temperature ranging between 5-6 Kelvin. The modern measurement of the cosmic microwave background is about 2.7 Kelvin.

English poet Lady Emmeline Stuart-Wortley in her poem 'The Maiden of Moscow' used the term outward space in 1842. Alexander von Humboldt used the expression of outer space as an astronomical term in the year 1845. H.G Wells later popularized the term in 1901. John Milton's Paradise Lost in 1667 first used the term space, a shorter form of outer space.

THE MODERN MEASUREMENT OF THE COSMIC MICROWAVE BACKGROUND

Redshift

| 0.5 | 1 | 2 | 0 |

| 6 | 11 | 17 | 0 |

Distance (billions light-years)

EXPLORATION

For much of human history, people explored space through observations made from the Earth's surface. Initially, they did this through the naked eye and later with the telescope. Before the creation of reliable rocket technology, the closest humans came to reaching outer space came in the form of balloon flights. In the year 1935, the U.S Explorer II crewed a balloon flight, reaching a height of 22 kilometers. The year 1942 saw the third launch of the German A-4 rocket, which rose to a height of 80 kilometers. In 1957, Russia launched the R-7 rocket, with the unscrewed satellite Sputnik 1. The Russians followed this up by the first human spaceflight in 1961, when Yuri Gagarin became the first man to go to space. Frank Borman, Jim Lovell and William Anders in 1968 were the first humans to escape low-Earth orbit onboard the Apollo 8. The spacecraft achieved lunar orbit and reached a maximum distance of 377,349 kilometers from the Earth.

Russian spacecraft Luna 1 was the first of its kind to reach escape velocity and performed the first fly-by of the Moon in the year 1959. Two years later and Venera 1 became the first planetary probe to reveal the presence of solar wind. It also performed the first fly-by of Venus but contact was lost before it reached the planet. Mariner 2 successfully made a fly-by of Venus in 1962. The first fly-by of Mars was by Mariner 4 in the year 1964. From then on, unscrewed spacecraft successfully examined each of the Solar System's planets as well as their moons and many minor planets and comets. In August 2012, Voyager 1 became the first man-made object to leave the Solar System and enter interstellar space.

Picture of Soviet cosmonaut Yuri Gagarin

The lack or absence of air in outer space makes outer space an ideal location for astronomy at all wavelengths of the electromagnetic spectrum. The pictures taken from the Hubble Space Telescope allowing light from more than 13 billion years ago to be observed is further evidence of this theory.

The U.S Explorer II

10

However, not every location is space is ideal for a telescope. The interplanetary zodiacal dust emits a near-infrared radiation, which could mask the emission of faint sources such as extrasolar planets. Moving an infrared telescope past the dust can increase its effectiveness. In the same way, a site like the Daedalus crater located on the far side of the Moon, can shield a radio telescope from the radio frequency interference that usually hampers Earth-based observations.

Spacecraft without a crew are an essential technology for modern civilization. These devices allow direct monitoring of weather conditions, relay long-range communications like television, provide a means of precise navigation and allow remote sensing of the Earth. The latter role has a variety of purposes like tracking soil moisture for agriculture, prediction of water outflow from seasonal snow packs, detection of diseases in plants and trees and surveillance of military activities.

Russian spacecraft Luna 1

The deep vacuum of space is an attractive environment for certain industrial processes. Like asteroid mining, space manufacturing would require a large financial investment with little chances of immediate return. The costs of access to space has declined since the year 2013, partially because of reusable rockets like the Falcon 9, which have lowered access to space. With these new rockets, the cost to send materials into space remains high for many industries. In order to address these issues, concepts like fully reusable launch systems, non-rocket space launch, and momentum exchange tethers and space elevators have been developed.

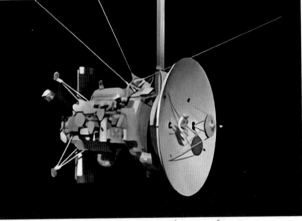

Model of an unmanned spacecraft

Interstellar travel for a human crew at present remains a theoretical possibility. The distance to the nearest stars means it would require new developments in technology and the ability to safely sustain crew for journeys that normally take several decades to complete. Some proposed interstellar propulsion systems include light sails, ramjets and beam-powered propulsion. More advanced systems could possibly use antimatter as a fuel source, reaching speeds currently inconceivable.

An A-4 rocket on display at Peenemunde, Germany

Light sail or solar sail is one possible mode of travelling through space

FUTURE

NASA's future will be a story of human exploration, technology and science. They aim to nurture the development of a vibrant low-Earth orbit economy that builds on the work done by the ISS. NASA engineers will develop new technologies and improve air transport at home to meet the challenges of advanced space exploration.

Commercial companies will play an increasing role in the space industry- launching rockets and satellites, transporting cargo and crew and building infrastructure in low-Earth orbit. NASA aims to be a global leader in scientific discovery and foster opportunities to turn new knowledge into things that help explore space further.

The United States is not the only country with lunar ambitions. China is planning a crewed mission to the Moon's South Pole by 2030, and has already successfully landed a robotic rover on the Moon's far side. India meanwhile launched a combined lunar orbiter, lander and rover on 22 July 2019, in a mission known as Chandrayaan-2.

The costs of building and launching spacecraft for future missions is a major obstacle organizations must overcome. One example of these innovations is the development of a new space capsule called Orion, managed by both NASA and the ESA. The vehicle is designed to take astronauts to and from the ISS and enable repeat landings on the Moon's surface.

As machines become increasingly capable of performing tasks independently, many organizations are looking to prioritize

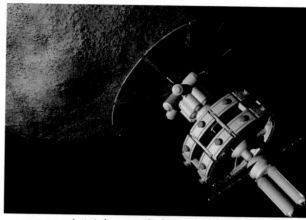

Artist's depiction of a futuristic spacecraft

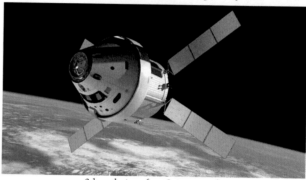

3d rendering of an Orion capsule

robotic over human spaceflight. These machines can handle specific tasks and can withstand the extreme conditions of space.

The Mars Curiosity Rover from NASA is a prime example of this. It launched on 26 November 2011 and landed on the surface of Mars on 5 August 2012. It explored the Martian landscape. NASA's Perseverance rover is the most recent rover to explore the Martian surface, having landed on the Red Planet in February 2021.

QUICK FACTS

Mars Curiosity Rover had its own Twitter account, updating millions of followers with its latest scientific observations.

Space Law

Space law is a body of law concerned with governing space-related activities. It encompasses both international and domestic arrangements, principles and rules. Parameters of space law include areas like space exploration, information sharing, new technologies and ethics.

Other fields of law like administrative law, intellectual property law, arms control law, environmental law, insurance lawn, criminal law and commercial law are also part into space law.

The origins of space law date all the way back to 1919, with international law recognizing each country's sovereignty over the airspace that is directly above their territory. During the Chicago Convention of 1944, the law was reinforced. The onset of domestic space programs during the Cold War helped to propel the official creation of space policy, initiated by the International Council of Scientific Unions. The launch of Sputnik 1 by the Soviet Union further spurred the United States Congress to pass the Space Act. This created the National Aeronautics and Space Administration, better known as NASA. Since space exploration needed to cross the transnational boundaries, it was during this era where space law became a field that was independent from traditional aerospace law.

Following the Cold War, the Treaty of Principles Governing the Activities of States in the Exploration and Use of Outer Space, including the Moon and Other Celestial Bodies or the Outer Space Treaty and the International Telecommunications Union provide the legal framework and set of principles and procedures about how space law operates. Further, the United Nations Committee on the Peaceful Uses of Outer Space or COPUOS, along with its Legal, Scientific and Technical Subcommittees, are tasked with debating issues of international space law and policy. The United Nations Office for Outer Space Affairs or UNOOSA serves as the secretariat of the Committee.

The Mars Curiosity Rover

RELATIVE SIZE ON THE SKY
Hubble legacy field   The Moon

30°   30°

Hubble Deep Field Mosaic revealing another part of the universe

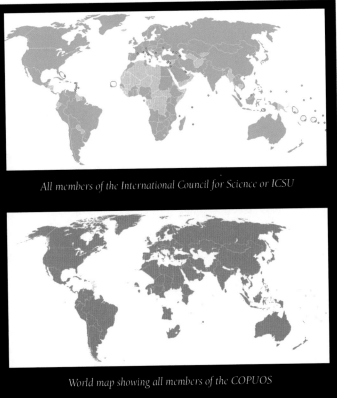

All members of the International Council for Science or ICSU

World map showing all members of the COPUOS

Challenges that space law will continue to face are four main categories: spanning across dimensions of domestic compliance, international cooperation, ethics and the advent of scientific innovators. Additionally, there are specific guidelines about the definition of airspace yet to be universally determined.

Regions of space

There is a partial vacuum in space. The various atmospheres define the different regions of space and 'winds' found within each region. These regions extend to the point where those winds give way to those beyond. Geospace extends from Earth's atmosphere to the outer edges of Earth's magnetic field, where it gives way to the solar wind of interplanetary space.

Interplanetary space extends to the heliopause, where the solar wind then gives way to the winds found in the interstellar medium. Interstellar space continues to the edges of the galaxy, whereupon it fades into the intergalactic void.

GEOSPACE

Geospace is the region of outer space found near Earth. This includes the upper atmosphere and the magnetosphere. The Van Allen radiation belts lie within the geospace. The outer boundary of geospace is the magnetopause, which form a kind of interface between the Earth's magnetosphere and the solar wind. Within the inner boundary is the ionosphere. The variable space-weather conditions of geospace is directly affected by the behavior of the Sun and the solar wind. The study of geospace is interlinked with the subject of heliophysics, i.e., the study of the sun and the way it influences the different planets of the Solar System.

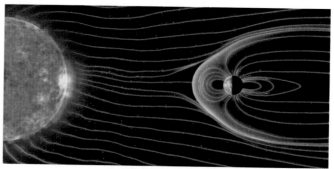

Rendering of a magnetotail

This creates Geomagnetic storms. Geomagnetic storms can disturb two regions of geospace; the radiation belts and the ionosphere. These storms increase fluxes of energetic electrons that could permanently damage satellite electronics, GPS location and shortwave radio.

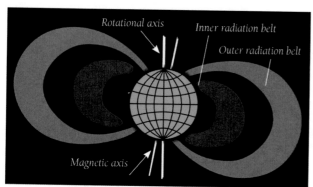

Cross section of the Van Allen radiation belts

The pressure from solar wind compresses the dayside magnetopause. The subsolar distance from the center of the Earth is marked at 10 Earth radii. On the night side, the solar wind stretches the magnetosphere, forming a magnetotail. The magnetotail can extend out to more than 100-200 Earth radii. For approximately four days of each month, the magnetotail shields the moon as it passes through this region.

Much of geospace consists of electrically charged particles at very low densities. Earth's magnetic field influences the movement of these particles. These plasmas form a medium where storm-like disturbance powered by the solar wind are able to drive electrical currents into Earth's upper atmosphere.

What Earth's magnetic field could look like

Magnetic storms are also a danger to astronauts, even when they are in low Earth orbit. The storms can also create the aurorae phenomenon seen at high altitudes in an oval surrounding the geomagnetic poles.

Although geospace meets the definition of outer space, the atmospheric drag within the first few hundred kilometers above the Karman line can still produce significant drag on satellites. This region of space has material left over from earlier crewed and un-crewed launches, creating a potential hazard to spacecraft. There are times when some of this space trash re-enters the Earth's atmosphere.

CISLUNAR SPACE

Earth's gravity keeps the Moon in orbit at an average distance of 384,403 kilometers. The region found outside Earth's atmosphere and extending out past the Moon's orbit is called cislunar space.

The Hill Sphere is the region of space where Earth's gravity is the dominant force against the gravitational force of the sun.

With deep space, there are different definitions as to where it starts. According to the United States Government and others, deep spaces is the region beyond cislunar space. The International Telecommunications Union responsible for radio communication defines the beginning of deep space at approximately five times that distance.

The aurora phenomenon, caused by Geomagnetic storms

INTERPLANETARY SPACE

Interplanetary space consists of the mass and energy, which fills the Solar System. This region is where all the other bodies in the Solar System, like planets, dwarf planets, asteroids and comets move. It stops at the heliopause, outside of which is where the interstellar medium begins.

The interplanetary medium includes interplanetary dust, cosmic rays and hot plasma from the solar wind. The density of this region is very low, decrease in inverse proportion to the square of the distance from the Sun. Magnetic fields and coronal mass ejections can often affect the region.

Artistic representation of interplanetary dust

QUICK FACTS

Before 1950, interplanetary space was thought of as either an empty vacuum, or made up of 'aether'.

What cosmic rays could look like

Since this region is a plasma, it exhibits characteristics of a plasma instead of a simple gas. For example, it carries the Sun's magnetic field with it, is highly electrically conductive and forms plasma double layers. Here, it is exposed to a planetary magnetosphere and exhibits filamentation, similar to what is seen in aurorae.

How the interplanetary medium interacts with planets depends on whether they have magnetic fields or not. Celestial bodies like the moon have no magnetic field and the solar wind can directly affect the surface. For billions of years, the lunar regolith has collected solar wind particles and so, studies of rocks from the lunar surface are valuable in studies of the solar wind.

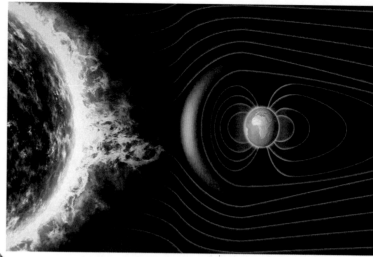

Image showing how the path of solar wind is deflected by Earth's magnetosphere

Study of lunar rocks can provide valuable insights into solar wind

High-energy particles from the solar wind affecting the lunar surface also cause it to emit faintly X-Ray wavelengths.

Planets that have their own magnetic field, like Earth and Jupiter are surrounded by a magnetosphere within which their magnetic field is dominant over the Sun's. This disrupts the flow of the solar wind, which travels around the magnetosphere. Material from the solar wind can 'leak' into the magnetosphere, causing the aurorae phenomenon and populating the Van Allen radiation belts with ionized material.

The cataclysmic explosion of a supernova produces an expanding shock wave, consisting of ejected materials that further enrich the medium. The density of matter in this region can vary greatly. The average is around 10^6 particles per m^3, but in cold molecular clouds can hold 10^8-10^{12} per m^3.

There are a number of molecules found within interstellar space. The total amount of molecules discovered through radio astronomy is steadily increasing at the rate of four new species every year. Large areas of higher density matter known as molecular louds are where chemical reactions can occur.

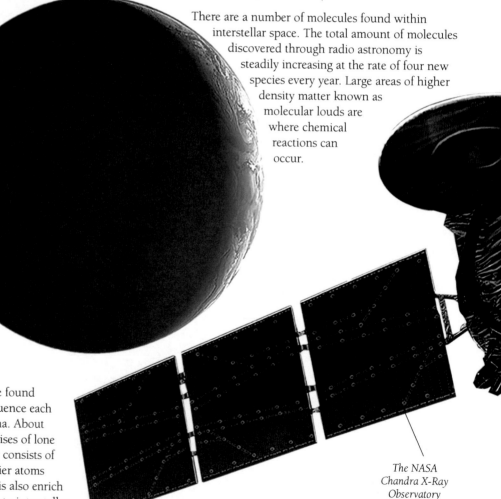

The NASA Chandra X-Ray Observatory

INTERSTELLAR SPACE

Interstellar space is the physical space found within a galaxy, lying beyond the influence each star has upon the encompassed plasma. About 70% of the mass of this region comprises of lone hydrogen atoms, while the remainder consists of helium atoms. Trace amounts of heavier atoms formed through stellar nucleosynthesis also enrich this region. These atoms are ejected into interstellar space by stellar winds.

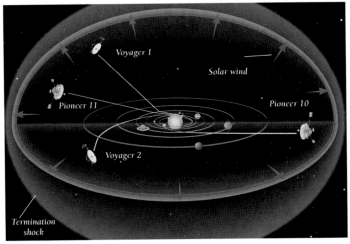

Picture of the NASA Voyager probe

These reactions include the formation of organic polyatomic species. Much of the chemical reactions occurring here are the result of collisions. Energetic cosmic rays pierce through the cold, dense clouds and ionize hydrogen and helium. An ionized helium atom can then split relatively abundant carbon monoxide and produce ionized carbon, which in turn can lead to more organic chemical reactions.

When stars are moving at high velocities, their stratospheres can generate bow shocks as they collide with interstellar space. For many years, astronomers believed that the sun had a bow shock. It was in 2012, where data from the Interstellar Boundary Explorer and NASA's Voyager probes indicated that the sun did not have a bow shock.

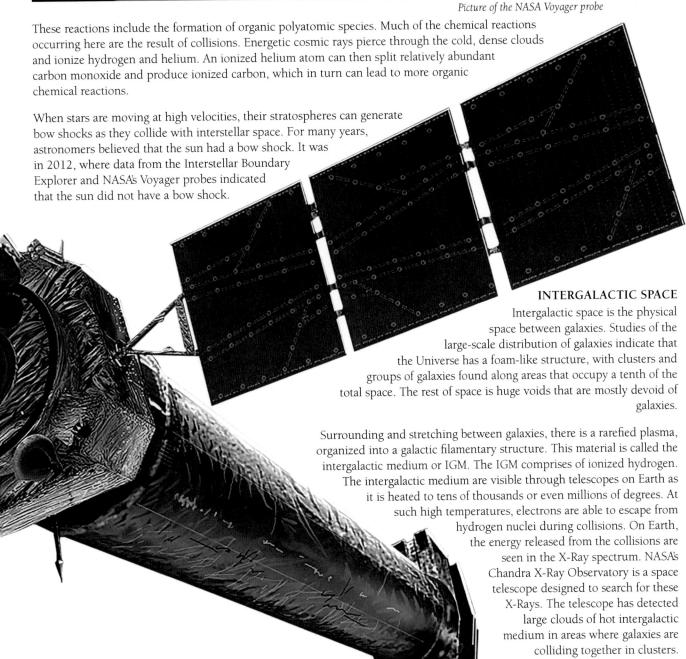

INTERGALACTIC SPACE

Intergalactic space is the physical space between galaxies. Studies of the large-scale distribution of galaxies indicate that the Universe has a foam-like structure, with clusters and groups of galaxies found along areas that occupy a tenth of the total space. The rest of space is huge voids that are mostly devoid of galaxies.

Surrounding and stretching between galaxies, there is a rarefied plasma, organized into a galactic filamentary structure. This material is called the intergalactic medium or IGM. The IGM comprises of ionized hydrogen. The intergalactic medium are visible through telescopes on Earth as it is heated to tens of thousands or even millions of degrees. At such high temperatures, electrons are able to escape from hydrogen nuclei during collisions. On Earth, the energy released from the collisions are seen in the X-Ray spectrum. NASA's Chandra X-Ray Observatory is a space telescope designed to search for these X-Rays. The telescope has detected large clouds of hot intergalactic medium in areas where galaxies are colliding together in clusters.

Plants in space

In spite of the harsh environment, several life forms are capable of withstanding conditions in space for extended periods. Species of lichen carried on the ESA BIOPAN facility survived exposure for ten days in 2007. Seeds of Arabidopsis thaliana and Nicotiana tabacum germinated after being exposed to space for 1.5 years. A strain of bacillus subtilis survived for more than 500 days when exposed to a simulated Martian environment.

A young plant aboard the ISS

The lithopanspermia theory suggests that rocks ejected into outer space from life-harboring planets can successfully transport life forms to another habitable world. Many scientists assume that such a scenario happened during the early history of the Solar System, with some microorganism-bearing rocks exchanged between Venus, Mars and Earth.

The growth of plants in outer space is the subject of much scientific interest. During the late 20th century and the early 21st century, plants were brought into space, to be grown in a weightless, but pressurized and controlled environment. In the context of human spaceflight, they can be consumed as food or even provide a stable atmosphere. Plants can also metabolize carbon dioxide in the air and produce oxygen, allowing them to control cabin humidity.

The first challenge to growing plants in space is being able to grow them without gravity. This runs into difficulties like the effects of gravity on root development, providing the right types of lighting and other challenges. In particular, the nutrient supply to the root as well as the nutrient biogeochemical cycles and microbiological interactions in soil-based substrates are very complex.

NASA plants to grow plants in space in order to feed astronauts and to provide some psychological benefits for long-term space flight. In 2017, in a plant growth device in the ISS, the 5th crop of Chinese cabbage was allotted for crew consumption, while the rest was saved for study.

QUICK FACTS

Space gardens are pressurized and controlled environments meant to grow plants.

A flower floating inside the ISS with Earth in the background

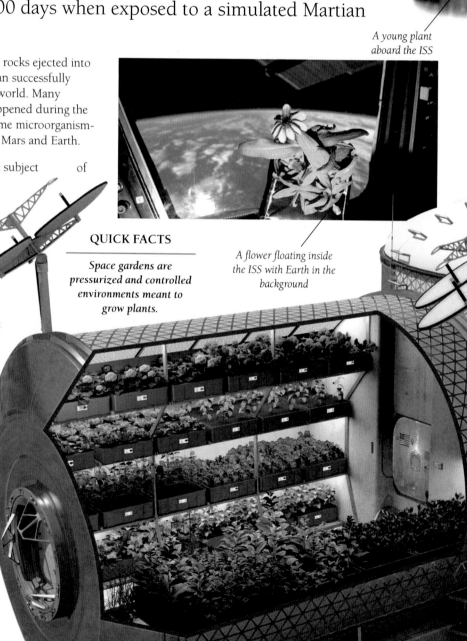

Animals in space

Animals in space was done to test the survivability of spaceflight, before human spaceflights were done. Later, other non-human animals were flown into space to investigate various biological processes and the effects of microgravity and space flight might have on them. To date, seven national space programs have sent animals into space. They are the Soviet Union, the United States, Iran, France Argentina, China and Japan.

The V2 rocket carrying Albert II

Since the 18th century, animals have often gone up in balloons and aircraft. In 1783, a sheep a duck and a rooster were sent up in the newly invented hot-air balloon. The balloon rose to a height of 3.2 kilometers and landed safely on the ground. The first animals in outer space were fruit flies. They were launched in a captured Nazi V-2 rocket on 20 February 1947. The flies reached a height of 108 kilometers and landed safely back by parachute.

Albert II was the first monkey to go into space on 4 June 1949. He reached a height of 134 kilometers but died on impact thanks to a parachute malfunction. The previous monkey, Albert I died when the V-2 rocket failed before reaching peak altitude. Albert III and Albert IV, two other monkeys also shared similar fates when their rockets failed.

A mouse launched on 15 August 1950 reached a height of 137 kilometers but died when the rocket disintegrated as a result of parachute failure. Following this, several other mice went into space during the 1950s. A total of 32 monkeys have gone into space. These include rhesus macaques, cynomolgus monkeys, squirrel monkeys and pig-tailed monkeys. Chimpanzees have also flown into space. Along with monkeys, a number of dogs went into space. In the 1950s, the Soviet Union launched 12 dogs in different sub-orbital flights. Stray dogs were used since they were thought to be capable of handling extreme cold. Laika, a stray mongrel was the first living being to orbit the Earth on Sputnik 2 on 3 November 1957. However, several hours of stress and heat led to her demise. On 2 July 1959, the Soviet Union launched two dogs and the first rabbit into space.

Illustration of different plants growing in a hypothetical base on Mars.

Albert II

Laika the space dog

The first spider web built in space

The Soviet Sputnik 5 was the first to return animals alive from orbit. The passengers were the dogs Belka and Strekla, a gray rabbit, 42 mice, two rats and fruit flies.

On 31 January 1961, Ham the Chimpanzee flew a Mercury capsule on a sub-orbital trajectory, three months before Alan Shepard's flight. Enos became the first chimp to orbit a Mercury spacecraft. Both chimps survived their flights.

The Sputnik 5 capsule along with models of Belka and Strekla

Ham the Chimpanzee before his flight into space

The French launched the first cat into space on 18 October 1963. Felicette had electrodes planted into her skin in order to transmit her condition. She reached a height of 160 kilometers before landing safely back down.

Between 1964 and 1966, China launched mice rats and dogs.

Russian space dogs Veterok and Ugolyok orbited for a record 22 days before landing safely on 16 March 1966. Their record for longest space flight by dogs still stand to this day.

In the year 1968, the Soviet Zond 5 was the first spacecraft to circle the moon. It carried a payload of two Russian tortoises, wine flies, mealworms, plants, seeds and bacteria. Zond 6 flew a similar trajectory later that year, but a malfunction on the return trip killed all the biological specimens onboard.

In the late 1960s, NASA launched a series of Biosatellites carrying insects, frog eggs, microorganisms and plants. The third and last biosatellite carried a pi-tailed monkey, but it died after landing from a heart attack.

After humans landed on the moon in 1969, animals in space became less important, but spacecraft still carried biological payloads. This included rabbits, turtles, insects, spiders, fish, jellyfish, amoeba and algae. In 1973, two female European garden spiders spun webs aboard the NASA space station skylab for 59 days. Biological payloads have also flown on NASA's space shuttle and the space stations of both Russia and America.

From 1966 to 1996, Russia launched a series of 11 Bion satellites. The Bion series resumed in 2013 with Bion-M1. Rodents on the spacecraft spent a month and experienced spaceflight conditions.

Enos is the third primate to orbit the Earth

Felicette, the first cat in space

Risks of travelling in space

Even at low altitudes in Earth's atmosphere, conditions are hostile to the human body. The altitude where atmosphere pressure matches the vapor pressure of water at the temperature of the human body is called the Armstrong line. It is named after American physician Harry G. Armstrong. At or above the Armstrong line, fluids in the throat and lungs boil away. Moreover, exposed bodily fluids like saliva, tears and liquids in the lungs boil away. As a result, human survival requires a pressure suit or a pressurized capsule.

Harry G. Armstrong, whom the Armstrong line is named after

In outer space, the sudden exposure of an unprotected human to very low pressure can cause pulmonary barotrauma, which is a rupture of the lungs. The large pressure differential between the inside and outside the chest is what causes this to happen. Even if the subject's airway is fully open, the flow of air through the windpipe can be too slow to prevent the rupture. Rapid decompression can also rupture the eardrums and sinuses. Bruising and blood seep can occur in soft tissues and shock can cause an increase in oxygen consumption, often leading to hypoxia.

Humans evolved for life in Earth gravity and exposure to weightlessness is shown to have detrimental effects on human health. Significant adverse effects of long-term weightlessness include muscle atrophy and deterioration of the skeleton. Other major effects include a slowing of cardiovascular functions, lower production of red blood cells,

balance disorders, eyesight disorders and changes in the immune system. Additional symptoms include fluid redistribution, loss of body mass, nasal congestion, sleep disturbance and excess flatulence.

The engineering problems associated with leaving Earth, developing space propulsion systems are subjects examined for over a century, and millions of hours of research were spent on them. In recent years, there has been an increase in research on how humans can survive and work in space for extended and indefinite periods of time. This question requires information from both physical and biological and physical sciences. Answering this question has now become one of the greatest challenges facing human space exploration.

Due to the hazards of a vacuum, astronauts have to wear a pressurized space suit while off Earth and outside their spacecraft

PHYSIOLOGICAL EFFECTS

Many of the environmental conditions experienced by humans during spaceflight are different from the conditions in which humans evolved. However, technology like spaceships and spacesuits can shield humans from the harshest conditions. The immediate needs for breathable air and drinkable water are addressed by a life support system, which supplies air, water and food. It must also maintain temperature and pressure within acceptable limits as well as deal with the body's waste products. Shielding against harmful external influences like radiation and micro-meteorites are also required.

Hazards like weightlessness are much harder to mitigate. Living in this type of environment affects the body in three ways: loss of proprioception, changes in fluid distribution and deterioration of the musculoskeletal system.

During takeoff and re-entry, space travelers can experience several times the normal gravity. An untrained person can usually withstand about 3g but can blackout at 4 to 6g. In order to overcome this, astronauts undergo G-force training and wear a G-suit, to help constrict the body and keep more blood in the head. Most spacecraft are built to keep g-forces within comfortable limits.

Human physiology is adapted to living within the atmosphere of Earth and a certain amount of oxygen is needed in the air we breathe. In case the body does not get enough oxygen, the astronauts are at risk of becoming unconscious and dying from hypoxia. In space, gas exchange of the lungs continues as normal but results in the removal of all gases from the bloodstream, including oxygen. After about 9 to 12 seconds, the deoxygenated blood reaches the brain and causes a loss of consciousness.

Close up picture of a micro-meteorite

Exposure to vacuum for more than 30 seconds is unlikely to cause any lasting physical damage. Animal experiments show that rapid and complete recovery is normal for exposures shorter than 90 seconds, while longer, full-body exposures are fatal and resuscitation has never been successful.

Another effect from a vacuum is a condition called ebullism. The condition results from the formation of bubbles in body fluids. Due to reduced ambient pressure, the steam may bloat the body twice its normal size and slow circulation. However, tissues are elastic and porous enough to prevent rupture even in this state.

An astronaut floating through space

Air force pilots also wear G-suits to protect their bodies when flying at high speeds

22

In a vacuum, there is no medium for removing heat from the body through conduction or convection. Loss of heat happens through radiation. This is a slow, process, especially for a clothed person, so there is no danger of freezing immediately. Rapid evaporative cooling of skin moisture in a vacuum can create frost, particularly in the mouth, but this too is not a significant hazard.

Without the protection of Earth's atmosphere and magnetosphere, astronauts are exposed to high levels of radiation. High levels of radiation can damage lymphocytes, cells that are vitally important to the immune system. The damage contributes to the lowered immunity astronaut's experience. In recent years, radiation is also linked to a higher incidence of cataracts in cosmic rays, greatly increasing the chances of caner over a decade or more of exposure. A NASA-supported study reports that radiation may harm the astronaut's brain and accelerate the onset of Alzheimer's disease. Though rare, solar flare events can give a fatal dose of radiation within minutes. It is thought that protective shielding and protective drugs could theoretically lower the risks to an acceptable level.

The crew living on the International Space Station are partially protected from the space environment by Earth's magnetic field, as the magnetosphere deflects the solar wind around the earth and the ISS. However, solar flares are still powerful enough to warp and penetrate the magnetic defenses, and so are still a hazard to the crew.

The most common problem experienced by humans in the initial hours of weightlessness is known as Space Adaptation Syndrome or SAS, commonly known as space sickness. It is similar to motion sickness and arises as the vestibular system adapts to weightlessness. Symptoms include nausea, vomiting, vertigo, headaches, lethargy and overall malaise. The first case of space sickness was in 1961. Since then, nearly half of the people who have flown into space suffer from this condition.

The International Space Station or ISS

Artistic depiction of space radiation

With the advent of habitable space stations, exposure to weightlessness has had some negative effects on human health. Humans are well-adapted to the physical conditions on the surface of the Earth and in response to weightlessness, various physiological systems begin to change. Though these changes are mostly temporary, some changes do have a long-term impact on human health.

Short-term exposure causes space adaptation syndrome. Long-term exposure causes multiple health problems, most notable being a significant loss of bone and muscle mass. These effects can impair an astronaut's performance and increase their risk of injury, reduce their aerobic capacity and slow down their cardiovascular system. Since the human body is mostly fluids, gravity tends to force them into the lower half of the body and there are systems in place to balance this. Without gravity, these systems still work, causing the redistribution of fluids into the upper-half of the body. This is the reason why many astronauts have a round face.

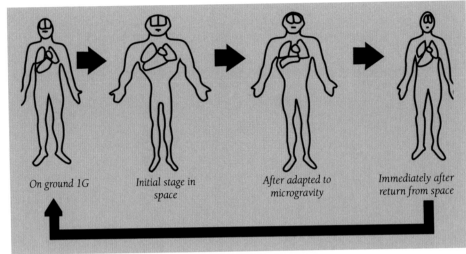

On ground 1G   *Initial stage in space*   *After adapted to microgravity*   *Immediately after return from space*

Cartoon illustration showing how micro gravity affects the fluid distribution in a human body

A major effect of long-term weightlessness involves the loss of bone and muscle mass. Without gravity acting on the human body, skeletal muscle is no longer needed to maintain posture and the muscle groups needed to move around in a weightless environment are different from those needed in terrestrial locomotion. In a weightless environment, astronauts put almost no weight on the back muscles or leg muscles used for standing up. These muscles start to weaken, eventually becoming smaller. At the same time, some muscles can atrophy rapidly. Without regular exercise, astronauts can lose up 20% of their muscle mass between five to eleven days.

The types of muscle fiber in muscles also change. Slow-twitch endurance fibers that help to maintain posture are replaced by fast-twitch rapidly contracting fibers that are not enough for any heavy labor. Advances in research on exercise, hormone supplements and medication can help to maintain muscle and body mass.

To counter the effects of long term of being in space, the ISS has two treadmills and various weight-lifting exercises to add muscle

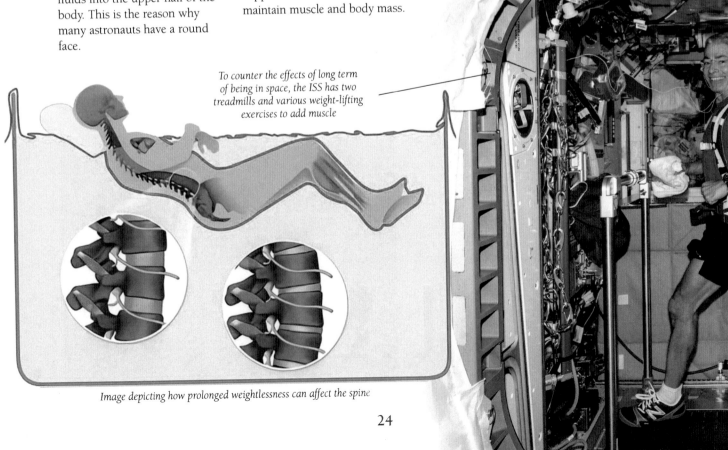

Image depicting how prolonged weightlessness can affect the spine

Bone metabolism also changes. The skeletal system is laid down in the direction of mechanical stress. However, in a microgravity environment, there is very little mechanical stress. Due to microgravity and the decreased load on the bones, there is a rapid increase in bone loss. The rapid change in bone density is dramatic, leaving bones frail and resulting in symptoms similar to osteoporosis.

On Earth, bones are in a cycle of being shed and regenerated through a system, which involves signaling osteoblasts and osteoclasts. In space however, there is an increase in osteoclast activity due to microgravity. This is problematic as osteoclasts break down the bones into minerals, which are reabsorbed by the body. Osteoblasts are not active with the osteoclasts, causing bone loss with no recovery. After a 3-4 month trip into space, it takes about 2-3 years to regain lost bone density. There are new techniques in development to help astronauts recover faster. Research into diet, exercise and medication may have the potential to aid the process of growing new bone.

QUICK FACTS

Astronauts subject to long periods of weightlessness wear pants with elastic bands attached between waistband and cuffs to help compress the leg bones, reducing osteopenia.

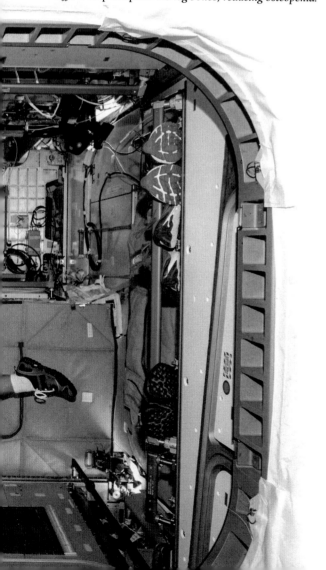

Studies of Russian cosmonauts provide data on the long-term effects of space on the human body

PSYCHOLOGICAL EFFECTS

The psychological effects of living in space are not fully understood, but analogies do exist on Earth, such as Arctic research stations and submarines. The stress on the crew, along with the body adapting to environmental changes can result in anxiety, insomnia and depression.

There is considerable evidence that psychological stressors are a major hurdle to optimal crew morale and performance. NASA's interest in psychological stress resulting from space travel began when their crewed missions began.

The amount and quality of sleep in space is poor thanks to variable light and dark cycles on flight decks and limited illumination during daytime hours in the spacecraft. The habit of looking out the window before sleeping can send the wrong messages to the brain, causing poor sleep patterns.

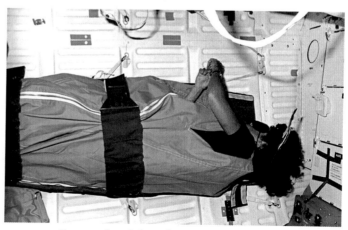

To prevent from drifting off, astronauts strap themselves down when going to sleep

Objects in space

DWARF PLANETS

Dwarf planets are worlds that are too small to be seen as full-fledged planets, but too large to fall into smaller categories. The International Astronomical Union defines a planet as being in orbit around the sun, has enough gravity to pull its mass into a rounded shape and has cleared its orbit of other, smaller objects. The last criterion is where planets and dwarf planets differ. A planet's gravity is able to attract or push away the smaller bodies that surround its orbit, while the gravity of a dwarf planet is not strong enough to make this happen.

Rendering of a comet

Dwarf planet Ceres

As of 2014, the IAU recognized five named dwarf planets: Ceres, Pluto, Eris, Haumea and Makemake. But these are not the only dwarf planets present. Other solar system bodies that are possibly dwarf planets include Sedna and Quaoar, which are small worlds found far beyond Pluto's orbit. 2012 VP113, an object that is thought to have one of the most distant orbits found beyond the estimated edge of the solar system. The object, DeeDee could also be a dwarf planet, according to observations made in 2017. According to NASA, scientists think that there may be more than a hundred dwarf planets still yet to be found.

Debate over the status of dwarf planets, particularly Pluto, remains a hot topic. The main concern stems from the requirement for a planet to clear out its local neighborhood.

Pluto

Pluto, Eris, Haumea and Makemake are all known as 'Plutoids' unlike the dwarf planetoid Ceres. A plutoid is a dwarf planet with an orbit outside that of Neptune.

These type of dwarf planets are also known as 'ice dwarfs' because of their miniature size and cold surface temperatures.

The outer planets have evidence of interaction with plutoids. Triton, the largest moon of Neptune, is likely a captured plutoid, and it is even possible the odd tilt of Uranus was the result of a collision with a plutoid. There are an unknown number of plutoid objects in the solar system that have yet to be given an official status.

Eris

Haumea

Halley's Comet on 8 March 1986

QUICK FACTS

A comet is so poorly structured, it is like a loose snowball

COMETS

Comets are small, frail and irregularly shaped heavenly bodies. Most are made up of frozen gas. However, some are composed of frozen gas and non-volatile grains. Comets typically follow very strict paths around the sun. They also become most visible when they cross the sun. This also applies to people who see comets through telescopes. When a comet nears the sun, it becomes very visible because of the sun's radiation and starts to sublime its volatile gases, which blows away small bits of the solid material the comet has.

Another feature of the comet is the long tail. This is a result of materials breaking off and expanding. They expand into an enormous escape atmosphere called the coma. With the comet travelling so fast, these materials are forced behind the comet, resulting in a long tail of dust and gas.

Comets are cold bodies. They can be seen thanks to gases that glow in the sunlight. Scientists believe all comets were formed from material in the outer part of the solar system. Compared to planets, comets are very small. They can be anywhere from 750 meters to 20 kilometers in diameter. Lately, scientists have been finding proof that there are comets 300 kilometers in diameter or greater.

The nuclei are solid, persisting of ice and gas. Most nuclei have rock similar to the rock found on Earth. The nucleus looks black in color because it is made up of carbon compounds. Since a comet's nuclei is so small, they are difficult to study from Earth.

The oldest comet on record is the Halley Comet. There are Chinese records of this comet dating as far back as 240 BC. Sir Edmund Halley predicted in 1705 that a comet which had appeared in 1531, 1607 and in 1682 would return in 1758.

Halley predicted the date on which the comet would return using Kepler's Third Law of motion.

Portrait of Sir Edmund Halley, a British scientist

ASTEROIDS

Asteroids are rocky metallic objects that orbit the Sun but are too small to be planets. They are known as minor planets. Asteroids range in size from 1000 kilometers down to the size of pebbles. Sixteen asteroids have a diameter of 240 kilometers of greater. They have been found inside Earth's orbit to beyond Saturn's orbit. Most asteroids are found within a main belt that exists between Mars and Jupiter. Some asteroids have orbits that cross Earth's path and some have even hit Earth in the past. One of the best preserved examples is the Barringer Meteor Crater found in Winslow, Arizona.

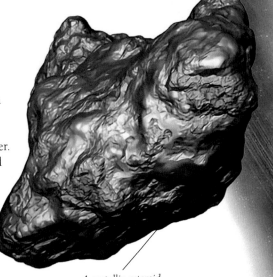

A metallic asteroid

Asteroids are material left over from the formation of the solar system. One theory suggests that they are the remains of a planet destroyed in a massive collision long ago. Most likely, asteroids are material that never coalesced into a planet.

Because asteroids are material from the early solar system, scientists are very much interested in their composition. Spacecraft flying through the asteroid belt have found that the belt is quite empty and the asteroids are separated by very large distances. Before 1991, the only information obtained on asteroids was through Earth based observations. Then, on October 1991, asteroid 951 Gaspra was visited by the Galileo spacecraft and became the first asteroid to have hi-resolution images taken of it.

Astronomers have studied a number of asteroids through Earth-based observations. Several notable asteroids include Toutatis, Castalia, Geographos and Vestia. Most of these asteroids were seen during close approaches to the Earth. Asteroid Vesta was seen by the Hubble Space Telescope.

According to expert testimony in the United States Congress in 2013, NASA would need at least five years to prepare before a mission to intercept an asteroid could be launched.

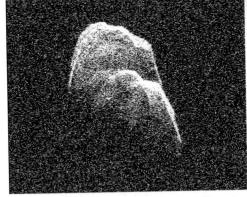

A meteor in the night sky

Image of asteroid Toutatis, taking by the Goldstone's Solar System Radar

Diagram of the Solar System's asteroid belt

28

METEOROIDS

Meteoroids are the smaller objects in orbit around the sun. Most of them come from comets that lose gas and dust when they approach the sun. Others are basically small asteroids. There is no exact diameter to help distinguish an asteroid from a meteoroid. The vast majority of all meteoroids are just a few millimeters and less in size. The smallest, and by far the most numerous ones have sizes of small dust particles and are called micrometeoroids. They do not leave any visible trace behind when they enter the Earth's atmosphere.

Meteoroids are usually categorized as iron or stony. As the name implies, iron meteoroids are made of about 90% iron, stony meteoroids are made up of oxygen, iron, silicon, magnesium and other elements.

Most meteoroids come from the asteroid belt, having been perturbed by the gravitational influences of planets, but others are particles from comets, giving rise to meteor showers. Some meteoroids are fragments from bodies such as Mars or the Moon that were thrown into space by an impact.

Meteoroids travel around the Sun in a variety of orbits at different speeds.

When meteoroids intersect with Earth's atmosphere, they are likely to become visible as meteors. If meteoroids survive the entry through the atmosphere and reach Earth's surface, they are called meteorites. Meteorites are transformed in structure and chemistry thanks to the heat of entry and the force of impact. NASA has produced a map showing the most notable asteroid collisions with Earth and its atmosphere from 1994 to 2013, from data taken by U.S. government sensors.

Illustration of a meteor shower

The entry of meteoroids into Earth's atmosphere produces three main effects: ionization of atmospheric molecules, dust that the meteoroid sheds and the sound of passage. During the entry of a meteoroid into the upper atmosphere, an ionization trail is created, where the air molecules are ionized by the passage of the meteor. These trails can last up to 45 minutes at a time.

A meteor shower happens due to the interaction between a planet and streams of debris from a comet or another source.

QUICK FACTS

If all the asteroids in the main asteroid belt was gathered into a single object, the object's diameter would be less than half of the Moon.

Neptune

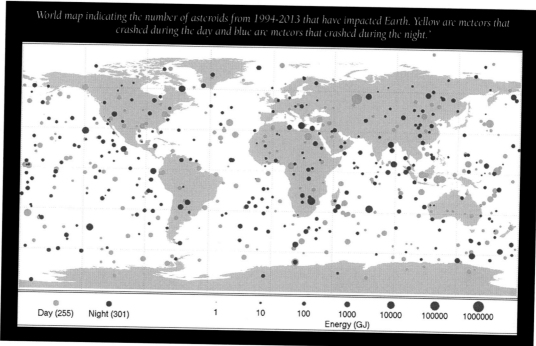

World map indicating the number of asteroids from 1994-2013 that have impacted Earth. Yellow are meteors that crashed during the day and blue are meteors that crashed during the night.'

| Day (255) | Night (301) | 1 | 10 | 100 | 1000 | 10000 | 100000 | 1000000 |

Energy (GJ)

GALAXIES

A galaxy is a gravitationally bound system of stars, stellar remnants, interstellar gas, dust and dark matter. Galaxies range in size from dwarfs with just a few hundred million stars to giants with one hundred trillion stars, each one orbiting its galaxy's center of mass.

Galaxies are categorized according to their visual morphology. They are divided into the following as elliptical, spiral or irregular, but there are many sub-categories within each classification. Many galaxies are thought to have supermassive black holes at their center. The Milky Way's central black hole has a mass four million times greater than the sun. As of March 2016, GN-z11 is the oldest and most distant observed galaxy, with a distance of 32 billion light years from Earth and observed as it existed 400 million years after the Big Bang.

Until the early 20th century, it was widely believed that the Milky Way was the only such structure in the Universe. Around the middle of the 18th century, German philosopher Immanual Kant proposed 'Island Universes' that were similar to the Milky Way and that populated the Universe. Sir William and Caroline Herschel were the first to systematically catalogue the night sky, they catalogued around 2,500 objects, including spiral nebulae that seemed to have a similar structure to the Milky Way.

The galaxies in the universe are changing through secular evolution, mergers and interactions. Galaxies in the early universe that have not formed stars yet are known as 'proto-galaxies.' These galaxies usually contain just dark matter and gas. It is theorized that some proto-galaxies may yet still exist, and there could be a class of dark galaxies that do not have the conditions required to form stars. These galaxies are solely made of dark matter. Astronomers and astrophysists are actively investigating the theory of galaxy formation.

Andromeda Galaxy, the closest neighbor to the Milky Way Galaxy

Image of elliptical galaxy ESO 325-G004

The Pinwheel Galaxy is an example of a spiral galaxy

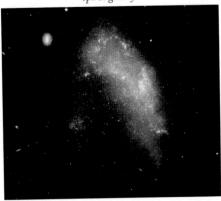

NGC 1427A is an example of an irregular galaxy

STARS

A star is an astronomical object made up of a luminous spheroid of plasma and held together by its own gravity. The sun is the nearest star to Earth. Many other stars are visible to the naked eye from Earth during the night, appearing as a multitude of fixed luminous points in the sky due to their immense distance from Earth. Historically, the most prominent stars were grouped together into constellations while the brightest ones have proper names. Astronomers assembled star catalogues that identify the known stars and provide standardized stellar designations. The observable universe contains an estimated 1×10^{24} stars, but most are invisible to the naked eye from Earth, including all stars outside our galaxy, the Milky Way.

Cluster of stars in the night sky

For most of its active life, a star shines due to the thermonuclear fusion of hydrogen into helium in its core, releasing energy that traverses the stars interior and then radiates into outer space. Almost all naturally occurring elements heavier than helium are formed by stellar nucleosynthesis during the stars lifetime. Near the end of its life, a star can also contain degenerate matter. Astronomers can figure out the age, mass, chemical composition and many other properties of a star by observing its motions through space, its luminosity and spectrum respectively.

The total mass of a star is the main factor that determines its evolution and eventual fate. Other features of a star, like its diameter and temperature, changes over its life, while the stars environment affects its rotation and movement.

A star's life begins with the gravitational collapse of a gaseous nebula of material composed mostly of hydrogen, helium and trace amounts of heavier elements. When the stellar core is dense enough, hydrogen is converted into helium through nuclear fusion, releasing energy in the process.

The Sun is the nearest star to Earth

The rest of the stars interior carries energy away from the core through radiative and convective heat transfer processes. A star with a greater mass than the Sun will expand into a red giant, when the hydrogen fuel in its core is exhausted. As the star expands, it throws a part of its mass into the interstellar environment, to be recycled later as new stars. Meanwhile, the core becomes a stellar remnant, a white dwarf, a neutron star, or a black hole

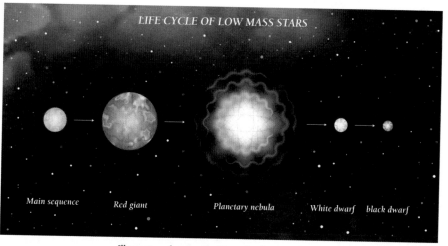

LIFE CYCLE OF LOW MASS STARS

Main sequence   *Red giant*   *Planetary nebula*   *White dwarf*   *black dwarf*

Illustration showing the life cycle of a typical star

31

BLACK HOLES

A black hole is a region of space-time where gravity is so strong, nothing, not even light can escape from it. The theory of general relativity predicts that a sufficiently compact mass can deform space-time and form a black hole.

Scientists think the smallest black holes formed when the universe began. Stellar black holes are made when the center of a very big star falls in upon itself or collapses. When this happens, it causes a supernova. A supernova is an exploding star that blasts part of the star into space.

Black holes have three layers, the outer and inner event horizon and the singularity. The event horizon of a black hole is the boundary around the mouth of the black hole, which light cannot escape. Once a particle crosses the event horizon, it cannot leave. Gravity is constant across the event horizon.

The inner region of a black hole is called as the singularity, the single point in space-time where the mass of the black hole is focused.

Scientists cannot see black holes the way they see stars and other objects in space. Instead, astronomers must rely on detecting the radiation black holes emit as dust and gas are drawn into the dense creatures. However, supermassive black holes, found in the center of a galaxy, are hidden by the think dust and gas around them, which can block the telltale emissions.

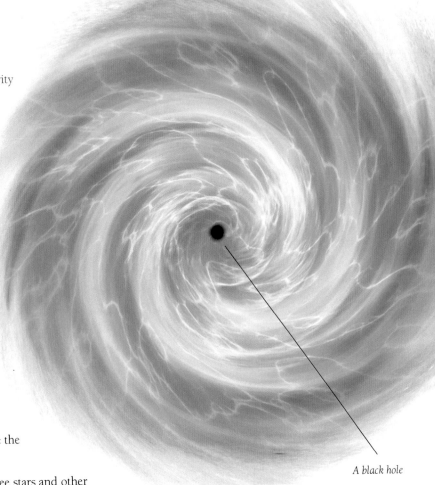

A black hole

Sometimes, as matter is drawn toward a black hole, it ricochets off the event horizon and is hurled outward, rather than being tugged into the maw. This creates bright jets of material, travelling at near-relativistic speeds. Though the black hole remains unseen, these powerful jets are viewable from greater distances.

The Event Horizon Telescope's image of a black hole released in 2019 was a monumental feat, needing two years of research even after the images were taken. This was due to images taken by multiple telescopes produced an astounding amount of data, too large to transfer through the internet.

A spiral galaxy being torn apart by a black hole

Drawing of a supermassive black hole found in the center of a galaxy

Made in the USA
Middletown, DE
11 January 2025

69332217R00020